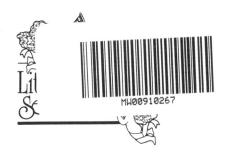

The Christmas Story

Text
Sr. Karen Cavanagh, C.S.J.

Illustrations
Rita Goodwill

Cover Illustration
Michael Letwenko

THE REGINA PRESS
New York

A VERY SPECIAL WOMAN

In the small village of Nazareth there lived a young woman whose name was Mary. Her parents, Joachim and Anne, knew that Mary was a special gift from God. She was filled with the love of God.

When she was very young, Mary went to temple school where she learned of God's promise and plan. As she grew older, she listened to God's word and prayed often. As she went about her work each day, she dreamed of her future and of Joseph, whom she would marry.

One day while she prayed, God's angel came to her and said: "You are full of grace! The Lord is with you!... You will have a son whose name will be Jesus. He is the Son of God."

Mary said: "I will do what God wants."

A VERY SPECIAL MAN

Mary was engaged to be married to Joseph, who was a carpenter in the village of Nazareth. Every day he worked in his shop where he made wooden furniture and wagons. The people were glad to buy Joseph's goods.

Joseph was a loving and sincere young man. He, too, thought often about God's promise and plan as he prayed with the other men who went to the temple to pray. He also dreamed of his future and of Mary, whom he would marry.

Once he dreamed God's angel told him that Mary's baby was God's child. The angel said: "Do not be afraid... Mary's child is the Son of God!" Joseph would marry Mary and Jesus would be a son to him.

Shortly after their wedding the Roman emperor wanted a count of all the people. Everyone had to return to the family's hometown to be counted.

Joseph belonged to the family of King David, whose hometown was Bethlehem.

At once Mary and Joseph left for Bethlehem. The town was crowded and noisy. People and animals filled the busy streets.

Because the town was so crowded, Joseph and Mary could not find a place to sleep. They were so tired and Mary thought her baby would soon be born. Someone told them of a cave that was outside of town. It was used to shelter animals. In this place, Mary and Joseph could rest. This very ordinary place would become...

A VERY SPECIAL PLACE

A VERY SPECIAL BABY

The time for the baby's birth had come at last. On that first Christmas day, Jesus was born. His mother wrapped Him warmly and laid Him on the soft hay. Joseph looked with love as they adored their new baby. They remembered the words: "He shall be the Son of God."

During that night some shepherds were watching their sheep in a field close by. They were poor people who would be part of God's promise and plan. God's angel appeared and said: "Do not fear. I have wonderful news. In Bethlehem, David's hometown, a child has been born. This child is Christ the Lord."

The angel said: "You will find the child wrapped in swaddling clothes and asleep in a manger."

As the shepherds wondered what this angel's message meant, more angels came and the whole sky was filled with a beautiful light. They sang: "Glory to God in high heaven and peace to all people on earth."

The shepherds looked about in amazement at the magnificent sight. One of them stood up and said: "Let us all go to Bethlehem and find this child of whom the angels speak."

The shepherds hurried to the cave
and the stable at Bethlehem. There
they found Mary, Joseph and the
baby. It was just as the angel had said.
In David's hometown had been born
Christ the Lord.

All the townspeople wondered at this event of which the shepherds told. They told of the angels and of the baby who was the Christ. They told of Mary, His mother.

The shepherds praised and glorified God for all that they had seen and heard. Mary quietly kept these things in her heart.

A VERY SPECIAL CHILD

Mary and Joseph began to understand that their baby was a very special child. All parents think their babies are special, and truly every baby is unique and special, but Jesus' parents knew their child was fulfilling God's plan and promise.

Eight days after He was born, Mary and Joseph gave their child the name of Jesus. This name means Savior and was given to Mary by the angel.

Sometime later Joseph took Mary, his wife, and Jesus, his son, to the temple in Jerusalem. There they made an offering to God and gave thanks for their special child. Because they were poor people, all that they could offer were two small birds.

There in the temple at Jerusalem was a just, holy and prayerful old man. His name was Simeon and he was filled with God's spirit. Simeon prayed in the temple often, reading the scriptures and waiting for God's plan and promise of a savior. God promised Simeon that he would not die before he had seen Christ the Lord.

As Joseph and Mary entered the temple, Simeon greeted them. When this old man saw the child Jesus, he knew he was looking at God's Son. He lifted Jesus into his arms and gave thanks to God. Simeon prayed: "Now, God, I can die in peace because my eyes have seen the Savior...This child will be a light to the whole world and the glory of your people...."

When Mary and Joseph took their son from Simeon's arms, they wondered at what Simeon had said. As they prepared to leave the temple, they came upon an elderly woman, Anna by name.

Anna was one of the prophets in Jerusalem. After her husband died, she could be found praying in the temple day and night. She even fasted for long periods of time. Her prayers were always begging God to send the Savior to the world.

As she was praying, Joseph and Mary passed by with their son. When the prophet, Anna, saw Jesus, she knew immediately that He was God's Son. Her heart was young again, and she hurried to tell all those who were also waiting and looking for the salvation of God's people. She told the news to everyone she met, saying: "The Son of God has come at last."

A VERY SPECIAL LIGHT

Far away in the east there were some astrologers who were studying the stars. On the night when Jesus was born, the sky was filled with light and they saw a bright new star.

They remembered the meaning: "A new star will appear in the sky when a great king is born to the Jewish people."

At once they started out to find the king. They traveled for months on camels carrying gifts for the baby. Day and night they followed the light of the star, which led them to Jerusalem.

In Jerusalem they found King Herod. Herod pretended to welcome them, but he was very angry. He thought:

How dare they search for a child king! I am the only king of the Jews.

King Herod's advisers told him that the prophets said the Savior would be born in Bethlehem. Herod told this to the astrologers and sent them off to find the Christ child. He continued pretending and said: "Look for the child Savior in Bethlehem. When you find him, come back and tell me where he is. I, too, wish to honor him and bring him gifts."

The astrologers again set out for Bethlehem. As they traveled in search of the Christ child, they did not know that King Herod did not have any plan to honor Jesus or offer him gifts. Herod was a very jealous man who planned to kill the child Jesus when he found him.

Not everyone was happy that Jesus was born.

The star led the way and at last the astrologers saw it stop above the cave. They went inside this poor dwelling and there they saw Jesus with His mother, Mary.

They knelt to honor the tiny king, and they opened their gifts of gold, incense and myrrh.

The astrologers went home another way because an angel told them in a dream that Herod wished to kill the child.

Joseph, too, received this warning in a dream. He told Mary what he had heard. They took their son and went to Egypt. They stayed there until Herod died.

After Herod died, Joseph and Mary returned to their own land with Jesus. There in Nazareth Jesus grew in wisdom and grace.

Each Christmas we remember again this wonderful story, which tells us that we are a very special people with whom God has come to live.